This book belongs to

Age

Favourite player

Prediction of Middlesbrough's final position this season

Prediction of Premier League winners this season

Prediction of FA Cup winners this season

Prediction of EFL Cup winners this season

Written by twocan

Contributors: Gordon Cox, Paul Dews, Alex Larkin & Rob Mason

A TWOCAN PUBLICATION

©2016. Published by twocan under licence from Middlesbrough FC.

ISBN 978-1-909872-84-4

PICTURE CREDITS
Varley Picture Agency, Action Images, Press Association, Mirrorpix

BORO'S GO

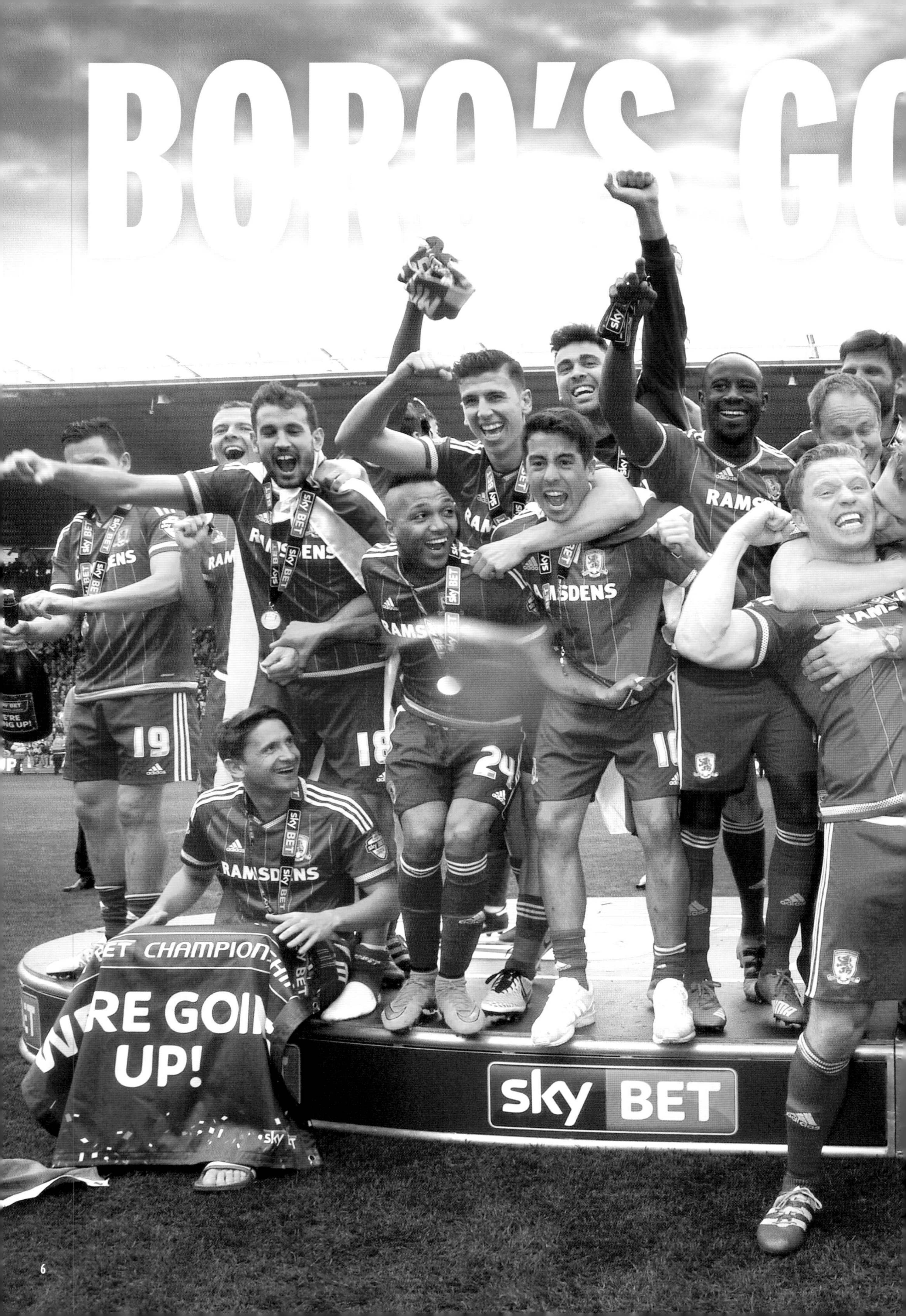

NG UP!

Fabio
DA SILVA
02

Position: **Defender** Nationality: **Brazilian** DOB: **09.07.90**

Fabio joined Boro in August 2016 from Cardiff. A fan favourite at the South Wales club, his only strike for the Bluebirds was a superb 25-yard goal on the half volley last season at the Riverside.

Dimitrios
KONSTANTOPOULOS
01

Position: **Goalkeeper** Nationality: **Greek** DOB: **29.11.78**

Part of the record-breaking defence that racked up nine consecutive league clean sheets last season, smashing a 30-year club milestone. Dimi kept an incredible 22 clean sheets throughout the campaign.

George
FRIEND
03

Position: **Defender** Nationality: **English** DOB: **17.10.87**

A popular figure among fans, Friend was named in the PFA Championship Team of the Year for both the 2014/15 and 2015/16 seasons for his adventurous performances from left-back.

The Squad 2016/17

Daniel
AYALA
04

Position: Defender **Nationality:** Spanish **DOB:** 07.11.90

Ayala was voted PFA Championship Fans' Player of the Year for his commanding displays last season and was awarded an extended deal this summer which will keep him at the Riverside until 2020.

Bernardo
ESPINOSA
05

Position: Defender **Nationality:** Colombian **DOB:** 11.07.89

Espinosa joined Boro this summer after his contract with Sporting Gijon expired. He was an integral part of Sporting's defence as the team won promotion to La Liga in 2015.

Grant LEADBITTER 07

Position: **Midfielder** Nationality: **English** DOB: **07.01.86**

Current captain and one of Boro's most consistent players, Leadbitter brings a wealth of experience and formed an uncompromising midfield partnership with Clayton last season.

Ben GIBSON 06

Position: **Defender** Nationality: **English** DOB: **15.01.93**

Gibson was an integral part of the record-breaking backline last season. He has represented England from U17 to U21 level with many thinking he will go on and play for the senior side.

Adam CLAYTON 08

Position: **Midfielder** Nationality: **English** DOB: **14.01.89**

Last season, Clayton was named Championship Player of the Month for December following a string of fine performances and Sky pundit Don Goodman named him his Championship Player of the Year!

Jordan
RHODES
09

Position: **Striker** Nationality: **Scottish** DOB: **05.02.90**

Rhodes joined Boro on deadline day in January 2016. He scored his first goal, a late leveller against MK Dons, just over a week later - the first of his six league goals last season.

Alvaro
NEGREDO
10

Position: **Striker** Nationality: **Spanish** DOB: **20.08.85**

A prolific striker, Negredo joined Boro on loan from Valencia this summer. He averages almost a goal every other game for his country and brings a wealth of experience to the squad.

Viktor
FISCHER

11

Position: **Midfielder** Nationality: **Danish** DOB: **09.06.94**

A Danish international, Fischer became Aitor Karanka's first signing this summer. He scored 11 goals in 39 appearances for Ajax last season, including one against Celtic in the Europa League.

Brad
GUZAN

12

Position: **Goalkeeper** Nationality: **American** DOB: **09.09.84**

US international Guzan joined Boro in July 2016 after an eight-year spell with Aston Villa. A veteran of 50 caps, he was awarded the Golden Glove when the US hosted the 2015 CONCACAF Gold Cup.

Tomas
MEJIAS

13

Position: **Goalkeeper** Nationality: **Spanish** DOB: **30.01.89**

Mejias was named in the Capital One Cup Team of the Tournament last season, particularly owing to his heroics as Boro beat Man Utd on penalties in the competition's round of sixteen.

Carlos DE PENA 16

Position: **Midfielder** Nationality: **Uruguayan** DOB: **11.03.92**

De Pena had spent his entire professional career playing for his boyhood club Nacional in Uruguay before joining Boro in summer 2015. He made six league appearances last season.

Marten DE ROON 14

Position: **Midfielder** Nationality: **Dutch** DOB: **29.03.91**

De Roon joined Boro from Atalanta in Serie A during the summer transfer window. He was the stand-out player with the Bergamo side during his single season at the Italian club.

Antonio BARRAGAN 17

Position: **Defender** Nationality: **Spanish** DOB: **12.06.87**

Right-back Barragan signed a three-year contract with Boro this summer. He joined from Valencia and made his first appearance during the pre-season trip to Marbella.

Cristhian STUANI 18

Position: **Striker** Nationality: **Uruguayan** DOB: **12.10.86**

Stuani was top scorer last season and had the honour of scoring against Brighton during the final game of the campaign - an iconic goal that would secure Boro's return to the Premier League.

Stewart DOWNING 19

Position: **Midfielder** Nationality: **English** DOB: **22.07.84**

A product of the Boro Academy, Downing completed his move back to Boro from West Ham in July 2015, signing a four-year contract. He was an integral part of the first team last season.

Julien
DE SART

23

Position: **Midfielder** Nationality: **Belgian** DOB: **23.12.94**

The club completed the signing of rising Belgian star, De Sart, from Standard Liege in January 2016. He made his Boro debut in Boro's 3-1 win over Cardiff City in February 2016.

Gaston
RAMIREZ

21

Position: **Midfielder** Nationality: **Uruguayan** DOB: **02.12.90**

Ramirez rejoined Boro on a permanent basis in the summer of 2016 after being a big hit and scoring seven goals while on loan last season. He also has a host of international experience.

Emilio
NSUE

24

Position: **Defender** Nationality: **Equatoguinean** DOB: **30.09.89**

Nsue is a versatile player, and though he has been employed primarily as a right-back by Boro, he has also featured on the right side of midfield, and can even play up front if needed.

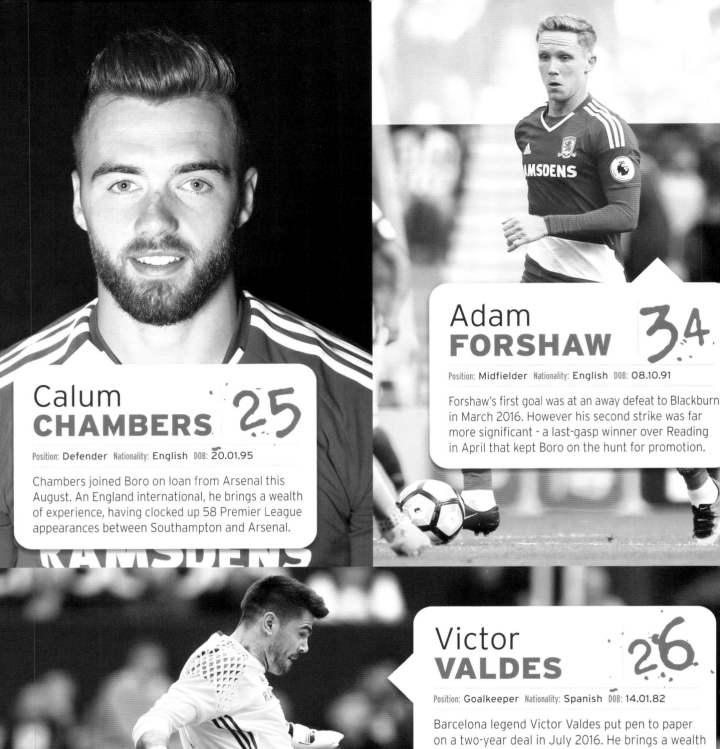

Calum **CHAMBERS** 25

Position: Defender   Nationality: English   DOB: 20.01.95

Chambers joined Boro on loan from Arsenal this August. An England international, he brings a wealth of experience, having clocked up 58 Premier League appearances between Southampton and Arsenal.

Adam **FORSHAW** 34

Position: Midfielder   Nationality: English   DOB: 08.10.91

Forshaw's first goal was at an away defeat to Blackburn in March 2016. However his second strike was far more significant - a last-gasp winner over Reading in April that kept Boro on the hunt for promotion.

Victor **VALDES** 26

Position: Goalkeeper   Nationality: Spanish   DOB: 14.01.82

Barcelona legend Victor Valdes put pen to paper on a two-year deal in July 2016. He brings a wealth of experience, having made over 500 appearances for Barcelona during a trophy-laden career.

Adama TRAORE 3.7

Position: Midfielder Nationality: Spanish DOB: 25.01.96

Traore joined Barcelona's youth setup as an eight-year-old and made his first appearance for the Spanish giants aged 17. He made the move from Villa to Boro this summer on transfer deadline day.

David NUGENT 3.5

Position: Striker Nationality: English DOB: 02.05.85

Nugent signed from Leicester City in August 2015. He was the top league goalscorer in the 2015/16 season with eight goals as Boro secured a return to the Premier League.

James HUSBAND 40

Position: Defender Nationality: English DOB: 03.01.94

Husband is a left wing-back and is a product of the Leeds United Academy. Since arriving on Teesside in July 2014, he has enjoyed two loan spells with Fulham, and a brief stint on loan at Huddersfield.

17

MIDDLESBROUGH
FOOTBALL CLUB
1876

RAMSDENS

8

Adam Clayton

Can you work out in which season each of these photos was taken?

There's a clue to help you with each one!

spot the season

A

Zenden celebrates with the Carling Cup trophy this season

B

Craig Hignett scores the first ever goal at the Riverside this season

C

All-time top scorer, George Camsell's first season at Boro

D

Middlesbrough v Man United
Boro finished 14th in Division One this season with Bosco Jankovic top scoring

E

Bernie Slaven was Boro's top scorer five seasons in a row. This was the fourth season!

ON OUR WAY!

An opening day draw at Preston offered no clue about what the season was to produce.

A win for the second year in succession at Oldham in the League Cup was followed with a first league win, a comfortable 3-0 success at home to Bolton, and it looked as though Boro's season was up and running.

But a draw at Derby was followed by a home defeat against Bristol City. Nerves were settled with seven straight wins, including every one of five games in September, a month that started and ended with comfortable points gained against MK Dons and Leeds.

October wasn't as profitable. It wasn't until the fourth game that winning form returned as Boro came from behind to win 3-1 at Wolves. The best game of the season to that point however came in that month as Boro beat Manchester United 3-1 on penalties after the sides drew 0-0 in the League Cup at Old Trafford. Defeat at Hull proved to be the only setback of a month that brought three wins as Boro kicked on in November.

A defeat by Everton in a League Cup quarter-final tie was the last of the year as Boro closed out December with four wins and a draw and a win at Brighton (the Seagulls' first defeat of the season) ensured they were top at Christmas.

A 2-0 home win over Derby was just one of two wins in January, but February was better, unbeaten in five, including a first ever visit to Stadium MK.

Defeat at Charlton late in March set alarm bells ringing, but Boro won the next six and drew the next four and that ten game unbeaten run, ending with a draw against a Brighton side who could also have been promoted automatically, took Boro back into the Premier League.

Saturday 7 May 2016 - a day that will live forever in the memory of Boro fans everywhere and the day that Aitor Karanka led the club back to the Premier League.

Seven years of top flight exile were put to an end on the final day of a pulsating Sky Bet Championship season as a 1-1 draw with the Seagulls at the Riverside was enough to win promotion on goal difference.

Weeks of to-and-fro and jockeying with Burnley and Brighton over the automatic promotion places came down to this; the mouth-watering prospect of a winner takes all showdown at the Riverside.

Burnley had secured their promotion with victory at home to QPR five days earlier, but Bo and Brighton had to wait. The previous year's heartbreak at Wembley was thrown on the backburner and the Riverside turned into a cauldron of immense noise in the build-up.

Boro knew that a single point would be enough to get them over the line and having already amassed over 88 that season plus the home advantage, fans were confident and in high spirits.

A sea of red and white greeted the teams as referee Mike Dea led both sets of players down the tunnel and the volume was positively deafening. Karanka's side flew out of the blocks an Brighton looked like startled rabbits in headlights amidst the blaze of the soon to be triumphant Teessiders.

It didn't take long for the roof to lift off. With just 19 minutes played David Nugent squared a Gaston Ramirez cross to Cristhian Stuani who turned the ball into the back of David Stockdale's net to send the stadium into raptures.

The home side continued to press and it looked as though a second would surely come as chances to double the advantage were squandered. Hearts were in mouths when Da Stephens managed to loop a header past Dimi Konstantopoulos on 55 minutes, but it took just four minutes for the hero to turn villain at the Riverside.

Stephens went over the ball with studs shown and clashed with Ramirez, scything a slice into the playmaker's leg, ending his afternoon. Mike Dean showed the Brighton man a straight red card and Stephens marched off down the tunnel.

Nerves were frayed and tension rose as late pressure from the Seagulls had the game stretched. Promotion was all but confirmed when Brighton's Bruno had a deep cross in a crowded box gathered by Dimi.

That was that. The whistle went and Boro had done it. Fans stormed the pitch and Aito Karanka was in tears after two-and-a-half seasons of hard work had finally paid off.

Boro were back and back with a bang.

HERE WE GO!

23

Club or Country?

Can you work out which team each set of clues is pointing to.. they could be Premier League, Championship or international.

1.

2.

3.

4.

5.

6.

7.

8.

9.

ANSWERS ON PAGE

Gaston Ramirez 21

A
Captained Arsenal to the European Cup Winners' Cup win in 1994

B
Hull City played thei home game here before moving to the KC Stadium

C
Crystal Palace's all-time top appearance maker

D
He scored two goals in Swansea's 5-0 League Cup final win over Bradford in 2013

E
He spent a successful seven-year spell at Chelsea

F
Man City retired squad number 23 in memory of this player

G
Burnley's top scorer last season

The answer to each clue begins with the corresponding letter of the alphabe

premier league

H — Led Bournemouth to promotion to the Premier League last season

I — Meaning of the latin phrase 'Consectatio Excellentiae' on Sunderland's crest

J — Honorary life president of Watford FC

K — Man City's Belgian captain

L — Man U have won the FA Cup 12 times, this man scored the winner in the 2016 final

M — Manager of Boro when they won the League Cup in 2004

MIDDLESBROUGH
FOOTBALL CLUB
1876

1 Start off with your feet on either side of the ball

2 Use one foot to roll the ball up your other leg

Make sure to roll the ball hard enough to give it some air

3

4 When the ball is in the air strike it with your heel

5 ...and flick it over your head!

Brazilian star striker, Neymar, is well known for his use of the rainbow kick on the pitch and regularly fools his opposition. The trick is an impressive show of skill which takes practice, practice practice!

TIP: Lean forward as you're doing the trick, this helps create space between you and the ball so you can strike it more easily.

A

Boro finished seventh in Division One this season with Alan Foggon top scoring

Can you work out in which season each of these photos was taken?

There's a clue to help you with each one!

B

The gates of Ayresome Park were padlocked as the club went into liquidation

C

Curtis Fleming and Robbie Mustoe celebrate promotion back to the Premier League

D

This season was the end of Stewart Downing's first spell at Boro

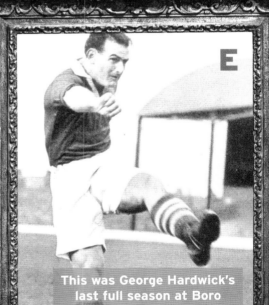

E

This was George Hardwick's last full season at Boro

spot the season

10
Alvaro
Negredo

On the Road

Do you know where every Premier League team play their home games?
Fill in the missing words and find all the grounds in the grid!

```
A I L T S T N M U I D A T S Y T I L A T I V
H N S V I C A R A G E R O A D J Q J Z K A O
F L F D U E K R A P N O S I D O O G R C L W
R M D I A M E G D I R B D R O F M A T S N H
I U H M E J F B J T K S E B I Z P K G C P I
V I C U Y L N G D R O F F A R T D L O K Y T
E D R I O R D M U I D A T S S E T A R I M E
R A S D E A L X V D R O I R 3 6 5 U A K E H
S T M A R Y S S T A D I U M K D F B N N R A
I S G T H M E U P T M H G L U C P Q I O W R
D 5 X S I A O J F G L A H Y O I S Y O R 3 T
E 6 F Y A E S M W E E G V W H P D M T B 5 L
S 3 E T I H A D S T A D I U M K F A P I 6 A
T T C R C O R V Q W X L D B Z R H I T A M N
A E H E V O T H G I L F O M U I D A T S L E
D B W B F Q E P S N R O H T W A H E H T C P
I M D I N K N B 5 6 3 T M U S F E N B A G K
U P Q L H L O N D O N S T A D I U M R G J W
M V S A O R M U I D A T S R E W O P G N I K
```

Team	Ground	Team	Ground	Team	Ground
Arsenal	_____ Stadium	Leicester	King _____ Stadium	Sunderland	Stadium of _____
Bournemouth	_____ Stadium	Liverpool	_____	Swansea	_____ Stadium
Burnley	____ Moor	Man City	_____ Stadium	Tottenham	_____ Hart ____
Chelsea	_____ Bridge	Man United	Old _____	Watford	_____ Road
Crystal Palace	_____ Park	Middlesbrough	_____ Stadium	West Brom	The _____
Everton	_____ Park	Southampton	St _____'_ Stadium	West Ham	_____ Stadium
Hull	KC _____	Stoke	_____ Stadium		

DANGER MEN

ARSENAL
LUCAS PEREZ

Signed from Deportivo La Coruna for a reported £17m just before the closure of the transfer window, 'Lucas' is a good fit for the Gunners. A player who looks to play 'one-two's' in and around the box the 28-year-old has played in Ukraine and Greece as well as Spain. Barcelona and Atletico Madrid were amongst his victims as he struck 18 times in 37 games last season, the best of his career so far.

BURNLEY
ANDRE GRAY

Having fired Burnley back into the Premier League in his first season at Turf Moor, 25-year-old Gray showed he intended to carry on in fine style in the Premier League with an early season goal in a sensational win over Liverpool. Wolverhampton born Andre came to the Clarets via Brentford who he'd joined after his goals brought Luton Town back into the Football League.

CRYSTAL PALACE
CHRISTIAN BENTEKE

Crystal Palace invested a club reco £27m in Belgium striker Christian Benteke in the summer, potential add-ons possibly adding another £5m to that fee. Class costs and the Eagles have a top class forward in Benteke who after beginning in Belgian football scored 49 goals in 101 games for Aston Villa before a £32.5m move to Liverpool where he netted 10 times in 42 games.

BOURNEMOUTH
CALLUM WILSON

Speed merchant Wilson made his name with his hometown team Coventry, costing the Cherries £3m in 2014. Having helped them into the Premier League he hit an early season hat-trick against West Ham but then picked up an injury which ruined his season. This time round he is hoping to show his Bourne supremacy.

CHELSEA
MICHY BATSHUAYI

Antonio Conte made Michy his first signing for the Blues, splashing out £33m on the young Belgium international. Strong and quick, Batshuayi could be Stamford Bridge's new Didier Drogba and like Drogba lists Marseille as one of his previous clubs. He also impressed with Standard Liege and is excellent at linking up play as well as putting the ball into the back of the net.

MIDDLESBROUGH
FOOTBALL CLUB
1876

EVERTON
OMELU LUKAKU

ll only 23, Lukaku is a powerhouse
iker and probably the nearest
ng in the game to his boyhood hero
lier Drogba. Romelu emulated his
l by making Chelsea his first
glish club. A debutant with
derlecht when he had just turned
he excelled on loan from Chelsea
West Brom and subsequently
ved to Everton, the Toffees making
their record signing at £28m. For
gium he had scored 14 goals in 49
mes at the start of this season.

LIVERPOOL
SADIO MANE

The scorer of the quickest hat-trick
in Premier League history when he
took just 2 minutes 56 seconds to net
three times for Southampton against
Aston Villa in 2015! The Senegal
international speed merchant cost
Liverpool £34m last summer, shortly
after he'd scored twice against them,
quickly followed by a hat-trick
against Manchester City.

ULL CITY
IEUMERCI
BOKANI

ned just as the transfer window
sed in the summer on loan from
namo Kiev, Mbokani came to Hull
h experience of the Premier League
ving scored seven times on loan to
rwich last season. The 31-year-old
re international has played in five
untries and won six league titles
d as many cups.

LEICESTER CITY
JAMIE VARDY

Jamie Vardy is the reigning Footballer
of the Year and Premier League Player
of the Year. His hard work and dedication
has seen him rise from non-league
football to the dizzy heights of the
Premier League. Last season he helped
fire Leicester City to the top of the table
and himself into the England team.

MANCHESTER CITY
SERGIO AGUERO

As dangerous as any dangerman in the
Premier League 'Kun' Aguero is simply
a goal machine. He's fired City to two
Premier League titles and two League
Cups and started this season with six
goals in his first three games including
a Champions League hat-trick. Last
season his haul included a hat-trick
against Chelsea and five goals in a
blistering 20 minute spell against
relegation bound Newcastle.

Watch out for these dangermen when Boro meet their Premier League rivals...

MANCHESTER UNITED
ZLATAN IBRAHIMOVIC

There are many stars in the Premier League and Zlatan Ibrahimovic is as big as any of them. The Super-Swede has finally arrived in English football this season after playing in the Netherlands, Italy, Spain and France as well as his own country. He has won the league title in 12 of his last 13 seasons and had scored 392 goals in 677 games at the start of this season.

SOUTHAMPTON
SOFIANE BOUFAL

Southampton broke their transfer record to bring in 22-year-old Morocco international attacking midfielder Sofiane Boufal shortly before the summer transfer window closed. Boufal began his career with Angers and came to the fore last season with Lille where he played in the final of the French League Cup against PSG a week after scoring a brilliant hat-trick against Ajaccio.

SUNDERLAND
JERMAIN DEFO[E]

Harry Kane and Jamie Vardy were t[he] only English players to score more Premier League goals than Defoe la[st] season. Jermain's tally of 15 include[d a] hat-trick at Swansea when he claime[d] his second match ball of the campai[gn] having also scored three in a League Cup tie with Exeter. At the start of t[he] season Jermain was the last player [to] score a hat-trick for England and he will be looking for a return to the international fold now that his ex-Sunderland manager Sam Allardyce has taken over the national side.

MIDDLESBROUGH
ALVARO NEGREDO

A debut goal on the opening day of the season is likely to be the first of many for the man who, when at Manchester City, bagged hat-tricks in the Champions League and the semi-final of the League Cup. In between his spells in England, Negredo played for Valencia, a team he once scored four goals in a game against for Sevilla.

STOKE CITY
XHERDAN SHAQIRI

Swiss international who acrobatically scored one of the most spectacular goals at Euro 16 against Poland. Having won three league titles and a cup at the start of his career with FC Basel in Switzerland, he moved on to Bayern Munich with whom he won the Champions League in 2013, as well as the European Super Cup, the World Club Cup and two Bundesliga titles before moving on to another continental giant in Inter Milan before coming to Stoke.

SWANSEA CITY
BORJA BASTON

Swansea spent £15.5m in August to bring in Spanish striker Borja Baston. Last season he ripped up la Liga with goals in 29 starts and seven sub appearances with Eibar, including a goal away to Barcelona. In 2009 Baston won the Golden Boot by scoring five goals at the U17 World Cup and now he'll look to fulfil his potential in the Prem.

WEST BROMWICH ALBION
SALOMON RONDON

After taking time to get used to life in the Premier League, Venezuela international Salomon Rondon really looked to be getting to grips with the demands of English football by the end of his first season. Having come to Europe as a teenager in 2008 when he moved to Las Palmas his ability as a dangerman has since seen Malaga break their club record for him with Rubin Kazan investing £10m, Zenit St Petersburg a whopping £15.8m and West Brom a record £12m!

WATFORD
ODION IGHALO

Famed for his 'picture-goals' Odion has been with the Hornets since 2014. He scored 20 goals in his first season as Watford won promotion and scored 15 (plus a couple in the cups) in his first season in the Premier League when he won the League's Player of the Month award in December 2015. A Nigerian international, Ighalo played in Nigeria, Norway, Italy and Spain before coming to England.

TOTTENHAM HOTSPUR
HARRY KANE

The Premier League's top scorer in 2015/16 with 25 goals, Kane bagged 21 the year before (31 in all competitions). Now 23, Harry debuted for Tottenham in 2011 in a Europa League game with Hearts before loans with Leyton Orient, Millwall, Norwich and Leicester helped him develop his game. Now one of the most feared strikers in the league Kane started the season with five goals in 16 games for England.

WEST HAM UNITED
SIMONE ZAZA

Italy international Simone Zaza is on a year's loan to the Hammers who have the option of signing the 25-year-old from Juventus for a fee that would total over 20m Euros. Although infamous for his flamboyantly fluffed penalty against Germany at Euro 2016, Zaza is a real dangerman because as well as offering pace and strength he is also a threat in the air.

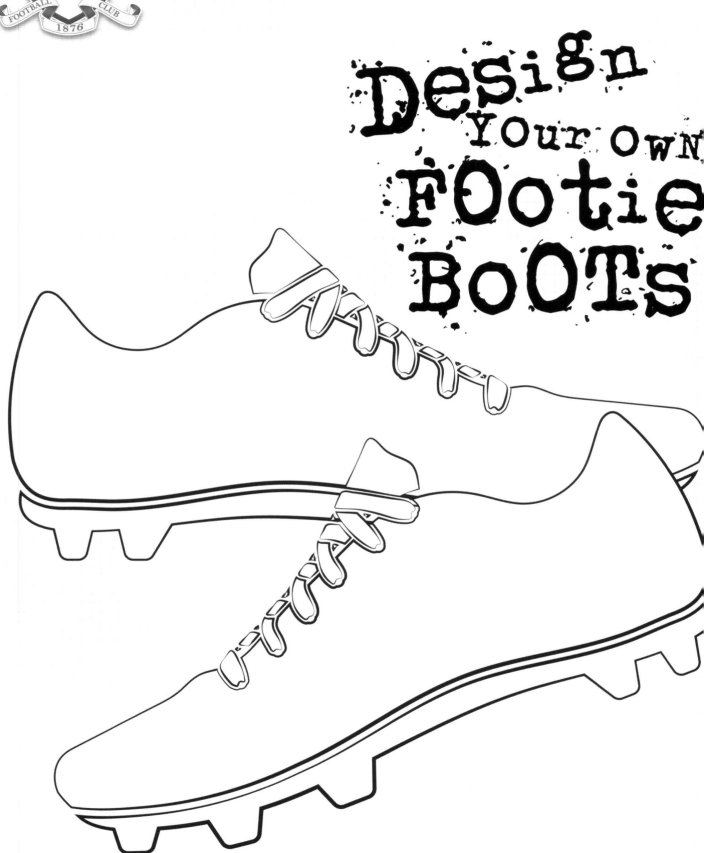

Design Your Own Footie Boots

35

David Nugent

Can you figure out the identity of these Boro stars?

A

B

Who are yer?

ANSWERS ON PAG

Quite often, they might have to play two matches within three or four days of each other and over the course of a season, regular players could play in the region of 50 games!

That would be a lot if they were simply running as a long distance runner does. In football though, that running is done with a mixture of short sprints from a standing start and runs of various lengths at differing intensities. On top of this, there is a lot of twisting and turning, often while someone is trying to pull the player back or even kick them. If they can cope with this, there is then the consideration that once the footballer has the ball, they have to use it, either with a telling pass or a shot on goal, while the opposition do all they can to stop them. Added to this is the fact that the thousands of fans watching in the stadium and the millions viewing on TV are only too ready to criticise them if they do not get it right.

To cope with all this, players have to be supremely fit so they have the stamina to last 90 minutes on a regular basis, and have the competitive edge to deal with opponents trying to stop them. Players also have to be careful to eat and drink the right things, get the right amount of sleep and keep themselves in tip-top shape.

In the summer when players return from a few weeks off, they do a lot of physical training to get themselves ready for the big kick-off. Once a few games have been played and they have, what players call, 'match-fitness', their aim is to maintain that fitness, but not over-do things.

Most players will train for two or three hours most days and do additional work in the gym, as well as perhaps doing pilates or yoga to help look after their bodies. Cycling and swimming can be useful too, but so is knowing when to simply rest, because the Premier League season is a long and gruelling campaign.

pre-season training

SKILLS: THE CRUYFF TURN

1 Draw back your foot as if you are going to kick the ball

2 Instead of following through, stop your foot over the ball ...

...and push it back behind your other leg while starting to turn your body.

3

4 Finish turning through 180° and head in the opposite direction.

5 Your unsuspecting opponent will be left standing wondering what just happened!

Johan Cruyff debuted his signature dummy at the 1974 FIFA World Cup. The trick is a brilliant manoeuvre to fool your opponent and change direction.

14

Marten
de ROON

N

West Ham's captain

O

Leicester's manager when they last won the League Cup in 2000

P

West Brom's first summer signing

Q

R

The manager who led the Foxes to the Premier League title

S

Captain of Stoke City

Signed for Sunderland as a striker and later became the club's chairman

The answer to each clue begins with the corresponding letter of the alphabet

premier league

ANSWERS ON PAGE 62

T

U
Tottenham's kit manufacturer

Everton's nickname

V
Stoke played their home games here before moving to the Britannia Stadium in 1997

W
Southampton's anthem

X
Arsenal's first summer signing

Y
Liverpool's club motto

Z
Chelsea's player of the year in 2003

While former Academy youngster Stewart Downing returned to the club from West Ham in a high profile transfer deal, the pre-season group which welcomed Downing, included a teenage hopeful taking the first steps in his career.

England youth international Dael Fry linked up with the senior squad for the first time last summer, impressing as he trained and played alongside the likes of Downing and fellow Teessiders Ben Gibson and Jonathar Woodgate during the club's pre-season games.

Ironically, it was an injury to Gibson, sustained during the penultimate warm-up game of the summer, which led to young Dael being called upon to make his first team debut in the opening game of the season, at Preston.

In a feisty Championship opener, Dael showed a matur beyond his 17 years as he slotted in alongside Daniel Ayala at the heart of the Boro defence for the first tim

It proved to be the first of Dael's eight appearances during the season and, although he had to wait until February before making his second start, he did so at Elland Road in a keenly contested clash against Leeds United and slotted in at the back as if he had been an ever present.

A handful of appearances followed for Dael before a summer of recognition saw him represent England Under 20s in the European Championships.

One to Watch

DAEL FRY

19

stewart
Downing

Fantastic

here are five members of Team GB hidden in the crowd.
an you find them all?

PLAYER OF THE YEAR

Adam Clayton

It was a clean sweep for midfielder Adam Clayton in terms of player of the year accolades for last season's promotion winning campaign.

The midfield man proved why Aitor Karanka had been so kee to sign him in the summer of 2014 by establishing himself as a key figure at the heart of Boro's push for the Premier Leag

Karanka joked after signing Clayton from Huddersfield that it was his flamboyant beard that had caught the e when, in all seriousness, it was the midfield man's neat tidy and determined approach that made him one of th most effective players in the Championship.

Having established himself alongside captain Grant Leadbitt during his debut season with the club, Clayton went on to feature in 43 of Boro's 46 Sky Bet Championship games and played a pivotal role in the promotion winning season.

Clayton scored his first Boro goal against his former club Huddersfield Town in November and went on to collect a stri of man of the match awards in televised games, notably in th 3-0 win against close rivals Brighton, the weekend before Christmas.

The midfielder's excellent form continued in th second half of the season with his industry and versatility shining through and while 13 yellow cards showed the combative edge to his game and cost him two suspensions, Clayton came o age in a team which clinched promotion, agains Brighton at the Riverside in May.

GOAL OF THE SEASON

The 2015/16 Goal of the Season was won by Southampton loanee Gaston Ramirez after Boro fans voted in their numbers on social media for the playmaker.

Ramirez made a tremendous impact upon his January arrival and stole the show on a number of occasions as Aitor Karanka's side marched to promotion from the Sky Bet Championship.

Gaston Ramirez

However, it was his one fine effort against Huddersfield Town at the Riverside Stadium on Tuesday 5 April that caught the eye of Teessiders everywhere.

It was the Uruguayan who carved out a breakthrough for Boro that night, when he twisted and turned in the box before winning a penalty on 32 minutes. Grant Leadbitter stepped up without hesitation for the spot kick and slotted it past Jed Steer in the Terriers' goal to fire Boro into the lead.

Just one minute later, Ramirez pounced on a loose pass by former Boro man Dean Whitehead and charged through midfield to find himself through on goal.

He threw a dummy to send Steer to the ground, rounded the keeper and blasted the ball into the roof of the net to double the home side's lead.

Though Boro's lead was already unassailable, our Goal of the Season wouldn't come until the second half when Ramirez placed the ball for a free-kick around 30 yards from goal.

A moment of magic from Ramirez saw the midfielder bend the ball with pace and accuracy past the goalkeeper who was helpless to stop it.

In a bid to find our best goal of the 2015/16 campaign, the club chose a shortlist of five for the fans to pick which would be a fitting winner.

Diego Fabbrini, two from Stewart Downing, Emilio Nsue and Ramirez all made the top five. Fans voted on Twitter and it was Ramirez who edged it – just beating Nsue to the crown.

34

Adam Forshaw

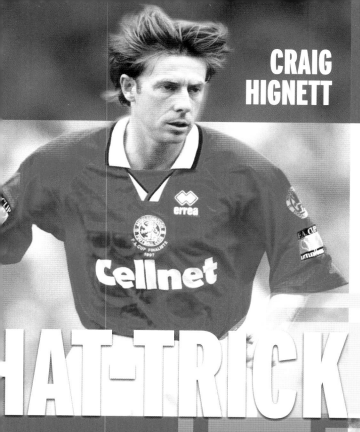

CRAIG HIGNETT

Middlesbrough 5 Brighton 0
21 September 1993

Scorer of the first goal at the Riverside, Craig Hignett is also the last Englishman to score four goals in one game for Boro - they came in this League Cup second round first leg tie at Ayresome Park.

A composed finish at the Holgate End saw Hignett convert a left-wing cross from Alan Moore with 15 minutes played.

He then scored three goals in four minutes to complete his hat-trick before half-time.

A sweeping six-pass move turned defence into attack as he cut in from the right to shoot low for his second, rounding off another break with a simple finish close to the goal line for his hat-trick. There was still time for his fourth before half-time, again scoring from close to the goal line. John Hendrie added a the fifth as Boro recorded what was then their biggest win in the competition.

HAT-TRICK

iddlesbrough 3 Liverpool 3
August 1996

...vanelli scored three hat-tricks for Middlesbrough, but his first was ... most memorable, coming on his debut after joining from Juventus ...o had just won the Champions League. It was the first time any player ... scored a hat-trick at the Riverside. This one came on the opening ...y of the 1996/97 season.

...t was then a record Riverside attendance of just over 30,000 watched the White ...ther, whose last goal had been in the Champions League final, score from the penalty ...t to equalise an opener from Stig Inge Bjornbye.

...n Barnes had restored Liverpool's lead before Ravanelli scored again, only to see ...bie Fowler put Liverpool into the lead for the third time. That lead lasted until ...anelli completed his hat-trick in the 81st minute.

...vent on to score two more hat-tricks, against Derby County and Hereford United.

FABRIZIO RAVANELLI

HEROES

JELLE VOSSEN

Millwall 1 Middlesbrough 5
6 December 2014

A first half hat-trick paved the way for a thumping win at The Den.

His first goal in Boro colours came on 21 minutes when a well-weighted ball over the top from Kenneth Omeruo set up the Belgian.

Boro had added a second with Patrick Bamford's fifth goal in six games before Vossen added his second on 33 minutes when stretching to turn home a cross from Adam Reach.

Just two minutes from half time, capitalising on a mistake in the centre of the Millwall defence caused by a George Friend header and Vossen flick, Bamford worked his way into a shooting position. His effort was blocked but the ball ran to Jelle Vossen who completed a 22-minute hat-trick when stroking in from 12 yards.

Former Boro striker Scott McDonald pulled one back before Kike completed the rout.

1 Start off by simply dribbling the ball

2 While moving in a forward motion, tap the ball with your leading foot...

3 ...and start turning your body in the opposite direction

4

5 As you're spinning, pull the ball back with your other foot while continuing to turn

6 Then keep moving forward!

Argentinian maestro, Maradona, is very well known for this move. It is brilliant for overcoming opponents and getting yourself into space, as while you are spinning you are putting your back to the defender and shielding the ball.

MIDDLESBROUGH FOOTBALL CLUB 1876

Can you work out in which season each of these photos was taken?
Here's a clue to help you with each one!

A
Boro finished fifth in Division Two this season with Brian Clough top scoring

B
The team celebrate promotion from Division Three this season

C
This was Tony Mowbray's last season at Boro until he would return as manager

D
Massimo Maccarone's famous diving header against Steaua Bucharest happened this season

spot the
season

E
Bryan Robson became Boro's oldest first team player this season at 39 years and 355 days

ANSWER ON PAGE 62

MIDDLESBROUGH FOOTBALL CLUB 1876

WILLIE MADDREN

Player of the Year in 1971, Haverton Hill born Willie was a classy defender who played 351 games for the club who he went on to manage.

JOHN CRAGGS

Hard tackling right back who played 486 times for Boro after joining from Newcastle, who he was subsequently transferred back to and had a testimonial against.

Hardwick's statue stands outside the Riverside. He played for Great Britain as well as England, played 166 times for 'Boro in a career interrupted by World War Two and cost a record fee for a defender when he moved.

GEORGE HARDWICK

TIM WILLIAMSON

Boro's record appearance maker. Williamson played 602 games for the club between 1901 and 1923. At 5' 9" England international 'Tiny' Tim was small for a keeper but he was special - he even scored two penalties in 1910!

DREAM

STUART BOAM

Tall and powerful centre-half who formed a superb partnership with Maddren, never more than in the 1973/74 season when Boro conceded just 30 goals in 42 games - only eight of them at home! Boam totalled 393 games for Boro.

PAUL GASCOIGNE

One of the most naturally talented English players of all time, Gazza debuted for Boro at Wembley as a sub in the 1998 League Cup final, after signing for a club record £3.45m. It was one of 44 games Paul played for the club.

GRAHAM SOUNESS

JUNINHO

Oswaldo Giroldo Junior cost £4.75m in 1995 and was worth every penny. The Brazilian thrilled the crowds and tortured opponents in the early years at the Riverside, when he combined absolute brilliance with a fierce will to win.

DAVID ARMSTRONG

Locally born England international who was Mr Consistency. Played 431 times for Boro, amazingly including 305 consecutive league appearances between 1973 and 1980.

WILF MANNION

Only Juninho rivals the Golden Boy for the title of Boro's best-ever player. A ball playing genius with a classic body swerve, England great Mannion played 368 club games, scoring 110 goals and making many more.

GEORGE CAMSELL

Camsell must have been good, to keep Clough, Boksic, Ravanelli and Hickton out of this team. He was! He scored 345 goals for Boro – 132 more than anyone else! In 1926/27 he got 59 in one season!

A dominant midfield enforcer who could also create, Scotland international Souness played 204 games and scored 23 goals, before commanding a record £352,000 move to Liverpool, where he'd make their 'Dream team' too.

There are too many footballs!

Work out which is the real ball in each photo.

A

B

WHAT BALL?

18

cristian Stuani

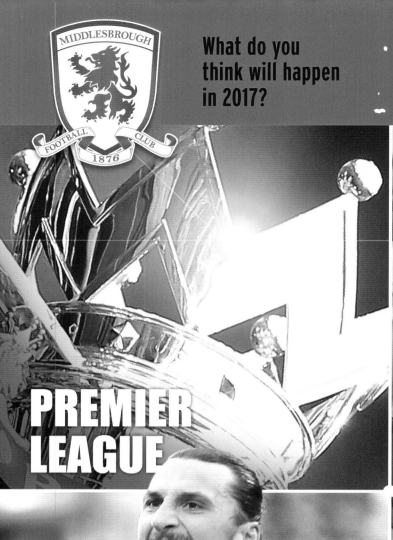

PREMIER LEAGUE

PREDICTION FOR PREMIER LEAGUE WINNERS:

Manchester United

YOUR PREDICTION:

PREDICTION FOR PREMIER LEAGUE RUNNERS-UP:

Chelsea

YOUR PREDICTION:

PREDICTION FOR CHAMPIONSHIP WINNERS:

Norwich City

YOUR PREDICTION:

PREDICTION FOR ALSO PROMOTED TO THE PREMIER LEAGUE:

Derby County & Brighton & Hove Albion

YOUR PREDICTION:

THE CHAMPIONSHI

PREDICTIONS

THE FA CUP

PREDICTION FOR LEAGUE CUP WINNERS:

Arsenal

YOUR PREDICTION:

PREDICTION FOR LEAGUE CUP FINALISTS:

Manchester City

YOUR PREDICTION:

PREDICTION FOR FA CUP WINNERS:

Middlesbrough

YOUR PREDICTION:

PREDICTION FOR FA CUP FINALISTS:

Liverpool

YOUR PREDICTION:

THE LEAGUE CUP

Answers

PAGE 19 · SPOT THE SEASON

a. 2003/04, b. 1995/96, c. 1925/26, d. 1980/81, e. 1989/90.

PAGE 24 · CLUB OR COUNTRY?

1. Hull City, 2. Newcastle United, 3. Spain, 4.Austria,
5. Wigan Athletic, 6. Tottenham Hotspur, 7. Iceland,
8. Arsenal, 9. Wolverhampton Wanderers.

PAGE 26
A-Z OF THE PREMIER LEAGUE

a. Tony Adams, b. Boothferry Park, c. Jim Cannon,
d. Nathan Dyer, e. Michael Essien, f. Marc-Vivien Foe,
g. Andre Gray, h. Eddie Howe, i. In pursuit of excellence,
j. Sir Elton John, k. Vincent Kompany, l. Jesse Lingard,
m. Steve McClaren.

PAGE 29 · SPOT THE SEASON

a. 1974/75, b. 1986/87, c. 1997/98, d. 2008/09, e. 1949/50.

PAGE 31 · ON THE ROAD

Arsenal - Emirates Stadium, Bournemouth - Vitality Stadium,
Burnley - Turf Moor, Chelsea - Stamford Bridge,
Crystal Palace - Selhurst Park, Everton - Goodison Park,
Hull - KC Stadium, Leicester - King Power Stadium,
Liverpool - Anfield, Man City - Etihad Stadium,
Man United - Old Trafford, Middlesbrough - Riverside Stadium,
Southampton - St Mary's Stadium, Stoke - bet365 Stadium,
Sunderland - Stadium of Light, Swansea - Liberty Stadium,
Tottenham - White Hart Lane, Watford - Vicarage Road,
West Brom - The Hawthorns, West Ham - London Stadium.

PAGE 38 · WHO ARE YER?

a. Adam Clayton, b. George Friend, c. Alvaro Negredo,
d. Antonio Barragan, e. Emilio Nsue, f. Adam Forshaw,
g. Viktor Fischer.

PAGE 44
A-Z OF THE PREMIER LEAGUE

n. Mark Noble, o. Martin O'Neill, p. Matt Phillips,
q. Niall Quinn, r. Claudio Ranieri, s. Ryan Shawcross,
t. the Toffees, u. Under Armour, v. Victoria Ground,
w. When the Saints go marching in, x. Granit Xhaka,
y. You'll never walk alone, z. Gianfranco Zola.

PAGE 48 · FANTASTIC

Nicola Adams, Bradley Wiggins, Greg Rutherford,
Jessica Ennis-Hill and Andy Murray.

PAGE 55 · SPOT THE SEASON

a. 1959/60, b. 1986/87, c. 1991/92, d. 2005/06, e. 1996/97.

PAGE 58 · WHAT BALL?

Picture A - Ball 6,
Picture B - Ball 6.